TELLING TALES

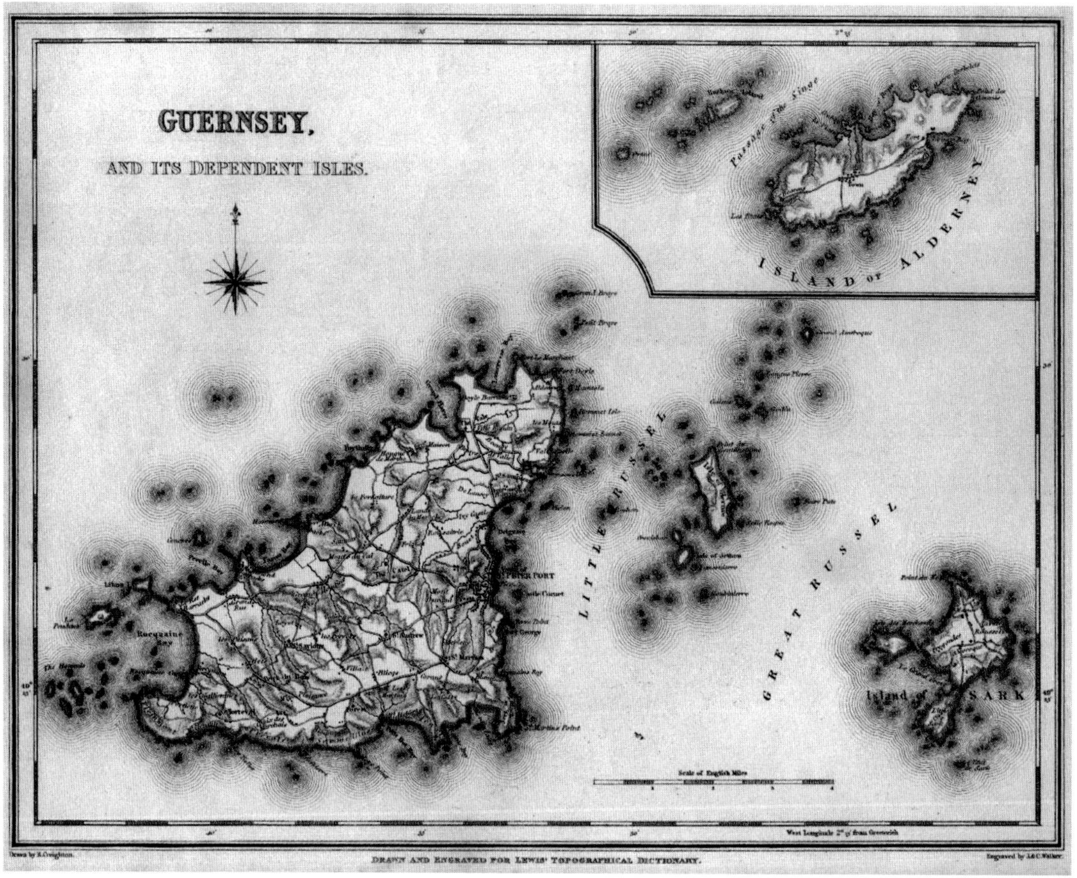

Guernsey, and its dependent isles. Drawn by R. Creighton and engraved by the admiralty engravers John and Charles Walker. Originally produced for the 'Topographical Dictionary' published by Samuel Lewis of Aldersgate in 1831.

Telling Tales

Guernsey news, views, ideas, snippets and gossip
from the early to mid-1800s

Compiled by Susan Ilie

ELSP

Published in 2009 by
ELSP
16A St John's Road
St Helier
Jersey JE2 3LD

Origination by Seaflower Books
Jersey

Printed by Cromwell Press Group
Trowbridge, Wiltshire

ISBN 978-1-906641-14-6

Contents

FOREWORD

The compiler of this miscellany of items spent considerable time reading newspapers, journals, periodicals and books spanning the early to mid 1800s.

She was intrigued by what she found and has diligently assembled for re-publication a range of material which will fascinate the reader and give an interesting insight into life in Guernsey in the 19th century.

Remember that the early decades of the 19th century saw considerable development in St. Peter Port, including improved streets and roads, handsome new Regency houses and the construction of the Royal Court, Elizabeth College, St. James, the Markets and the Arcade.

It was an era of great prosperity and confidence. Those roads, houses and public buildings have stood the test of time and we admire them today. However, over the years life in our community has changed dramatically. You will be able to judge from the material selected by Susan Ilie whether some of the changes have been beneficial.

Sir Geoffrey Rowland
The Bailiff of Guernsey

Acknowledgements

Thanks to Ciprian Ilie, Judy Porter, David Kreckeler,
Sir Geoffrey Rowland, Peter Sarl,
Roger Jones of Seaflower Books
and the ever helpful staff of the Priaulx Library.

Introduction

Guernsey has a rich past, there is no doubting that. The following collection of news stories, views, opinions, snippets and downright gossip brings to life the human aspect of living in the island in the early to mid nineteenth century. Prepare to be shocked and amazed as you read about real life stories and happenings.

Researching and putting together the contents of this book has been exciting and addictive. I hope you, dear reader, enjoy these tales as much as I did the first time my eyes saw them on their dusty pages.

I have left most of the language and grammar just as I found it, so it is not always perfect.

Thanks to those who in the past wrote down the news of the day and those whose findings on Guernsey were put into print, we can peer into the life and times of the island and its inhabitants all those years ago and understand what life was really like and how some things change and others are just the same today!

Susan Ilie

List of Illustrations

Reproduction, with the exception of the frontispiece, by permission of the Priaulx Library, Guernsey

Plate 14: Town of St. Peter's Port, Guernsey. Drawn from nature and on stone by Geo. Barnard, Day & Haghe, lithographers to the Queen. Originally published by M. Moss, bookseller, Guernsey

Plate 15: St. Pierre Port, Guernsey. C. Stanfield R.A., W. Pinden, engraver. Originally published by Smith Elder & Co., Cornhill, London

Plate 16: View from Clifton, Guernsey. On stone by L. Haghe, Day & Haghe lithographers to the Queen. Originally published by M. Moss, Guernsey.

Plate 17: View from Near the Cement Mill, St Saviours, Guernsey. Drawn by G. S. Shepherd, Day & Haghe lithographers to the Queen. Originally published by M. Moss, bookseller, Guernsey, 1840

Plate 18: The Terre and South Beach, Guernsey. Drawn by T. Compton, on stone by W. Gauci. W. Day lithographers to the King, London. Originally published by M. Moss, bookseller, Guernsey.

Plate 19: Petit Bo Bay, from behind the Mill, Guernsey. Drawn by T. Compton, on stone by W. Gauci. Originally published by M. Moss, bookseller, Guernsey, 1830.

Plate 20: Market Horses, St Peter Port, Guernsey. G. Barnard, lithographer. Originally published by M. Moss, bookseller, Guernsey, 1841.

Plate 21: Rocque du Guet, Cobo Bay. Drawn by J. Young from a sketch by T. Compton. Day & Haghe, lithographers to their majesties. On stone by W. Gauci. Originally published by M. Moss, bookseller, Guernsey, 1830.

Plate 22: Moulin Huet Bay, Guernsey. Engraved by A. Willmore. Burkit Foster artist.

Plate 23: Pier Head, St Peters Port. G. Barnard, lithographer. Day & Haghe, lithographers. Originally published by M. Moss, bookseller, Guernsey, 1841.

Plate 24: Silk programme for the Myers Grand Cirque Americain, held at the Castle Emplacement on Friday evening, June 29th, 1833

Plate 25: Saints Bay, Guernsey. Drawn from nature and on stone by G. Barnard. Day & Haghe, lithographers to the Queen. Originally published by M. Moss, bookseller, Guernsey.

1

Views and Opinions

The stranger who is unacquainted with the Island, its situation and extensive beneficial trade, and who, through the channel of a magazine, newspaper, or Gazetteer, has perhaps acquired a prejudice against it, as well as its inhabitants, constitution, and government, will be agreeably deceived when he finds that Guernsey, of which he conceived so mean an opinion, though of very small extent, has many valuable privileges and advantages that larger states do not enjoy; and, in point of situation and improvement, is one of the most fertile, flourishing, and best cultivated spots of ground in Europe.

The History of the Island of Guernsey, 1814
William Berry

Guernsey contains a considerable number of wealthy inhabitants, and there is a greater degree of refinement than in Jersey; but also a greater spirit of exclusiveness, which has excited the notice, and, in some cases, the ridicule of visitors. The best society is, in dress, manner, and language, on a level with society of the same rank in England. Party spirit is not so violent in Guernsey as in Jersey, nor do local political squabbles engross so much attention; the topics of conversation are more varied, and there is more amenity of manner and a more perfect understanding of the English language.

The Penny Cyclopaedia of the Society for the Diffusion of Useful Knowledge, Vol XI, London 1838

Provisions are plentiful and good, generally a little cheaper than in England.

Female servants ask six to twelve pounds a-year wages, and expect to be allowed to see their families and friends on Sundays, and occasionally to go out a merrymaking.

Gardeners' wages are rather high, and men are scarce. Indoor men-servants are almost unknown, and can with difficulty be found in the Islands.

Physicians' fees are extremely moderate; they usually send in an account, not charging by the visit. It is the cheapest place to be ill in I ever knew.

The Channel Islands, Pictorial, Legendary & Descriptive, 1857
Octavius Rooke

The natives of Guernsey keep themselves very secluded ; they have three classes of society — the sixties, the forties, and the twenties. The first, in their evening visiting carry a lantern with three lights ; the second, one with two ; and the third one.

Observations on Popular Antiquities, 1849
John Brand

Plate 1: The Quay

The visitor will be struck with the superior neatness of the cottages of Guernsey, as compared with those of Jersey. He will also remark the passion which the people of Guernsey have for flowers. Splendid geraniums may be seen trailed up the front of many of the cottages, and among the other flowers cultivated, we must not forget the far-famed Guernsey lily, the pride of the island, and the favourite of every gardener, and every cottager who has a bit of garden ground. The Guernsey lily belongs to the amarylideæ, or narcissus tribe of plants, and is a native of Japan. It is said to have been introduced into Guernsey by accident. A vessel, having some roots on board, was wrecked off the island, and these being washed on shore, grew up on the beach ; and the Hon. Mr Hatton, son of Lord Hatton, the then governor, being charmed by the beauty of the flower, set about its cultivation, and naturalised it.

A new and Pivtorial Description of England,
Scotland, Wales and the British Islands, 1847
Robert Sears

The true object of political government is the greatest happiness of the greatest numbers for the longest period of time.

The Guernsey and Jersey Magazine
February 1836

The character of the islanders is marked by a great deal of shrewdness; as to physical courage, they have given repeated instances of their bravery; and wherever they have been employed, at home or abroad, in public capacities, they have run the fair race of competition with their English, Irish, or Scotch brethren. There is a mixture of the French and English peculiarities in many of both the Jersey and Guernsey people, which is productive of good; the fiery irascible blood of Gaul is tempered with a due proportion of the phlegm of Albion, and the result is a determined, staid, but active individual, capable of the highest efforts to which his duties may call him. In honesty and truth the islanders are not surpassed.

History of the British Colonies, 1835
Robert Montgomery Martin

The robust and muscular character of the true English labourer is not seen in the working Guernseyman, nor is his acuteness of perception so evident; nevertheless, the Guernseyman, though slow, works well, and is intelligent.

The History of Guernsey, 1841
Jonathan Duncan

Plate 2: Grande Havre

The People of Guernsey

The women are very pretty; their faces of more classic form and feature than we meet commonly in England; and they all dress well. The men are of a more clumsy material; the beau is fat and foppish; the family man is very like the pictures of Mrs. Trollope's Americans. There is much beauty in the children; and an evident care is taken with their appearance, even among the lower orders; their hair is curled, and their clothes are in good taste; and one is puzzled to know when is this care given.

The Living Age, 1845
Eliakim Littell, Robert S. Littell

Note: 'Mrs Trollope's Americans' refers to the book *Domestic Manners of the Americans* by Mrs Frances Trollope published in 1832. This was the British author's first published and most important best-selling controversial book which recounts her travels during her four-year stay in America.

2

People

Yesterday, shortly after mid-day, William Fox, a sawyer, put a period to his existence by hanging himself in Mr. Moon's saw-pit, at the Piette. As soon as this unfortunate man was cut down, an attempt was made to bleed him, but the vital spark was extinct.

The Comet, Vol II No 2, April 6 1829

Note: Bleeding was used as a solution to many health ailments during the 1800s, but there were often serious consequences. For one thing, bleeding a person actually lessened the chances for a healthy recovery as it greatly weakened the patient. Doctors often bled patients until they fainted!

Sudden Deaths!

On Friday evening last, a young man, named JOHNS, after taking his supper, was taken ill suddenly, and expired immediately.

Yesterday morning, in jail, Mr WILLIAM BATISTE, in the prime of life.

The summons to all these was as sudden as unexpected.

– "in the midst of life we are in death!"

The Comet, Vol III No 27, September 27 1830

Sudden Death from Fright!

Monday last, a woman named Robilliard died suddenly under the following affecting circumstances. Her husband sailed on the preceding day on board of The Two Brothers, Capt. Humphreys, for Rio de Janeiro; and on Monday the Hannah Eliza Yacht, belonging to the Duke of Buckingham arrived here when some person went and told her it was The Two Brothers, put back. The poor woman believed it to be true and in the meantime imagined that her husband was not on board, and on this supposition, she frightened herself to that degree that it had such an effect as to deprive her of existence, a few minutes afterwards!

The Comet, Vol V No 44, August 31 1832

On Saturday morning last, as the cart belonging to Mr John Sarchet, jun., was going down High –Street, the horse in the shafts fell down in an apoplectic fit and expired on the spot; the shafts then came in contact with one of the windows of Mrs James Bodilly's shop, and smashed in two pains of glass and broke one of the bars of the sash frame.

The Comet, Vol VII No 13, May 12 1834

Plate 3: Castle Cornet

Shocking Accident

On Thursday last, an invalid named Grumly, whose business it was to fire the morning and evening gun at Castle Cornet, after having fired off the latter, proceeded to re-load the gun preparatory to the firing of the gun at sun-rise on the ensuing morning, when, very unexpectedly, the charge went off, and carried away all the fingers and thumb on his right hand, and dreadfully lacerated the bone of his right arm above the elbow....

The poor man walked from the top-battery, where the accident occurred, to his lodgings in the Castle, and from thence to the boat which was instantly prepared to bring him on shore in order to receive medical assistance. As soon as he was landed he was taken to the Military Hospital at Fort-George where his arm was amputated, close to the shoulder, by Dr O'Brien. Grumly has a wife and eight children.

There have already been several accidents of this sort, and it is to be regretted that the person whose business it is to attend to that matter is not strongly enjoined not to reload the gun till the morning, and vice versa.

The Comet, Vol VII No 59, October 20 1834

A man in an old house at the bottom of Fountain Street, fell down a flight of stairs and expired almost immediately.

The Comet, Vol VII No 68, November 21 1834

Sudden Death from Apoplexy

On Saturday last, about five o'clock in the afternoon, as James Naftel, aged 22 years, of the Petite Capelle, St Sampson's parish, was passing through George Street, New Town, he suddenly dropped on the ground and expired! He was taken up by Mr Shaw and Mr Francis and taken to Mr Angel's (dyer.) house, in the same street and placed in a chair till medical aid could be procured. Dr Hoskins was soon in attendance, but his services could be of no avail as the vital spark had already left its clay tenement. The deceased was afterwards seen by Drs Mansell and Roberts. We understood that Mr Naftel was subject to a flow of blood to the head, and it is supposed that he was seized in this manner on Saturday, when he was so suddenly deprived of his mortal existence.

The Comet, Vol VII No 91, February 9 1835

Plate 4: Fermain Bay

A Laughable Mistake

On Friday last, it being a calm and cloudy day, when no ripple brake upon the deep, nor was there a sound to be heard save a robin's lay, and the seafowl screaming for her prey; when all at once, some ladies who were enjoying themselves at Fermain's Bay, suddenly exclaimed that there was a man out at sea and in danger of being drowned, and with all the tender sympathetic feeling which is so peculiar to man's better portion, crying out with stentorian lungs "Oh haste! Oh quick, pull quickly, or the man will be drowned! See there! See there! He's now upon the bottom of a boat and sure he'll meet a watery grave"

The boat was launched upon the bosom of Old Neptune, and pulled with all the might and main of the navigator, who, looking about half-frantic, and amazed for the object said about to perish, still no boat, nor yacht, nor flapping sail could he espy in the situation described, but presently he heard a merry sailor-boy exclaiming "What old-un did you go to catch a porpoise by the tail"? roguishly enjoying the fun which the unaccountable mistake of the ladies had this occasioned at another man's expense.

The Comet, Vol VIII No 48, September 11 1835

A paragraph has found its way into some of our local papers stating that two "ladies" belonging to Fort George, had a very narrow escape from drowning, in the bathing machine at Fermain's bay last week, but we are authorised to state that no lady residing in the Fort has been placed in danger of her life from that quarter. It is true that two women thought proper to get into the machine for the purpose of bathing, but they do not live in the Fort, nor are they connected with it in any manner whatever. There are only three married ladies in the garrison, and we are very happy to hear that neither of them were exposed in the manner insinuated by our contemporaries.

The Comet, Vol IX No 32, July 14 1836

On Thursday last, the inhabitants, both in town and country, were not a little amused by the exhibition of a novel vehicle, namely – a boat, about 20 feet long, fixed on four carriage wheels, which was drawn by a small horse as far as l'Ancresse Common, and back again. It was fitted out with three masts, decorated with colours, and commanded by Captain SWINTON. This novel sight attracted an immense crowd of curious spectators around it, who made the air resound with their 'buzzas', to the amazement of those who were not previously informed of this unexpected land expedition! The voyage was performed in safety, but we have not heard that any new discovery was made, or that any new acquisition to science will be the consequence.

The Comet, Vol IX No 9, June 13 1836

Explosion of Gunpowder

An explosion of a small quantity of gunpowder took place in the house occupied by General SIR OCTAVIOUS CAREY, at Hauteville, on Friday night, under the following circumstances. It appears that two of Sir Octavus' sons had been sporting during the day and intended going out on the following morning, but finding that their powder was damp they spread it on a piece of paper and laid it on the dressing table, when a spark from the candle fell among the powder, when it immediately exploded, to the terror of the whole family, who were totally ignorant of the affair. –The consequence was, that the two young gentlemen were much burnt about the face – seventeen panes of glass were smashed to pieces, the fragments of which were thrown into the street – and the dressing table was very much damaged. Our informant states that there was about one pound of gunpowder. We are happy to hear, that notwithstanding this melancholy affair, the young gentlemen are not likely to have their sight affected by the accident.

The Comet, Vol X No 73, December 4 1837

Sudden Death

On Saturday last, Mr. JOHN KELEEN, mate of the Cutter Horatio, died very suddenly at the house he occupied on Fort Amherst. It appears that at about half-past six in the morning, he called up one of his daughters to prepare his breakfast, as he was to sail at half-past ten, which she did, when his wife said that she would get up also, as she had a pair of stockings to mend for him before he went, and whilst they were in conversation, he was seized with a fit of coughing, and reclining his head on his pillow, suddenly expired! Mr. HEPBURN, Surgeon, was instantly sent for, but his services were of no avail, the immortal spirit having quitted its clay tenement, before he reached the house of the deceased. An inquest was held in the Court House in the afternoon. Verdict – "Died by the visitation of God."

The Comet, Vol X No 73, December 4 1837

We are sorry to hear, that this afternoon, the corpse of Mr. DANIEL SARRE, of Mill-street, shoe-maker, was found floating near the neighbourhood of the Terres. We understand that he left home yesterday, and nothing was heard of him till be was discovered by Mr. VINCENT, as above stated. It is said that both his hands were tied together.

The Comet, Vol X No 101, March 12 1838

Yesterday between the hours of two and three o'clock in the afternoon, Mrs GAVET, wife of Mr James GAVET Jun. of the Forest parish, was found lying in the road leading to Mr GEORGE BREHAUT'S house, life being almost extinct; she was taken up by persons who happened to be passing that way and carried at the aforesaid house, where she shortly afterwards expired. It appears that the deceased was about eighteen years of age and that she had been confined three weeks since. That the Postman carried her a letter in the course of the morning from her husband, who is in America, and that at two o'clock in the afternoon she left her house in perfect health, with the view of going to her sister's house, Mrs BREHAUT, at a short distance, to inform her that she had just received a letter from her husband and that on the road her milk flew to her head which caused her death! When found, her milk was flowing out at her nostrils. A medical gentleman was called, but life was extinct, he gave it as his opinion that the rush of the deceased's milk to her head, was the cause of her death. The deceased was in very high spirits when she left her house, and just before that, she said to a relation of hers, "you'll mind my child whilst I go to chapel in the evening", little imagining that her earthly career was so near its final close. A Coroner's Inquest was held this morning at the Court House, when a verdict was given accordingly.

The Comet, Vol III No 84, 15 January 1836

Complaints have been made to us, that on Sunday mornings and Sunday afternoons, a number of boys are in the habit of congregating together on the South Beach, where they spend their time in gambling, instead of being at church, or some other place of worship. This should not be tolerated in a Christian country on the Lord's-day, and therefore we hope that our Police will not permit such assemblages in future, but will take steps to put an end to such disgraceful practices.

The Comet, Vol X No 102, March 15 1838

The Beaux and Belles seem to have had more than ordinary predilection for writing billets doux on this auspicious day. We understand that not less than three hundred and fifty Valentines were dropped into the Post-Office letterbox in this town ; and, as a matter of course, the letter-carriers were busily employed during the morning in delivering those precious epistles.

The Comet, Vol XI No 94, February 14 1839

On Wednesday last, the cutter Maria Ann, Captain OLLIVER, left London at three o'clock in the morning, and arrived here on Thursday afternoon at three o'clock – thus performing her passage in thirty-six hours. This is the shortest for a sailing vessel we have heard of.

The Comet, Vol XI No 15, May 14 1838

Plate 5: St Peter Port

PAINLESS OPERATION. – This morning, Mr B. COLLENETTE, Surgeon, administered æther to a lad of about 12 years of age, at Mr. GLEDSTAINES CAREY's residence, in the presence of Drs. CAREY, JOHN MAUGER and LE MARCHANT, and other gentlemen. The lad was soon and easily put under the influence of the æther, when Mr. GLEDSTAINES CAREY, in a very skilful manner, removed his thumb. The boy, on becoming conscious, laughed, and assured those assembled – which, indeed, was evident – that he had not in the slightest degree felt any pain; adding, that he would not object to undergo the operation a second time. His only wonder was, he said, as to what all those gentlemen could be about.

The Comet, Vol XIX No 96, February 11 1847

Last evening, Mr. PETER LE NOURY, fisherman, caught on his ground-lines off St. Martin's point, an immense conger. It measured 7 feet 6 inches long, 2 feet 4 inches in girt, and weighed 91 pounds. It was exhibited this morning, in one of the oyster shops in the fish market, at one penny per head. Many persons went to see it. In all probability, a larger fish of that kind has not been seen in this part of the world for very many years past.

The Comet, Vol XVI No 80, December 21 1843

Note

CURRENT RECORDS: CONGER

UK Record
Date Caught: 1991
Captor: M. Larkin
Location: Devils Point, Plymouth
Weight: 68-08-00lbs

Guernsey record
Date Caught: 20 September 2000
Captor: P. R. Carre
Location: Bec Du Nez
Weight: 65-14-10lbs

Plate 6: The Triumphant Return

The inhabitants round the vicinity of St. James' church are so much annoyed by the noise of the weathercock, as to prevent their sleep. The Rev. Gent who eats buttered lobsters, should reserve a little to grease it, the annoyance now complained of would then be prevented.

The Chit Chat, Guernsey, December 9, 1837

A certain young man, living in the vicinity of George Street, generally spends too much time at the toilet every morning, and particularly Sabbath mornings, which has often prevented his being at Chapel in time; we would by all means recommend him not to act in such a feminine like manner as he does, as there are certainly ladies enough in this Island to act their own parts; and he is more the object of ridicule by that part of the community than he is aware of. – Amice – will know to whom we refer.

The Chit Chat, Guernsey, December 30 1837

Unfortunate Circumstance

This day se'nnight, a young boy, aged about 12 years, named Edwin Bolt, had his right ear bitten entirely off, whilst standing in Bruce Lane, by a vicious horse belonging to William Brewer. This is an unfortunate circumstance for the poor boy.

The Comet, Vol IV No 9, May 23 1831

Note: 'Se'nnight' is an abbreviation of the fuller phrase seven nights, hence a week.

Plate 7: St James's

Allet versus Le Page

JANE ALLET actioned NICHOLAS LE PAGE, to pay her the sum of £20 for a breach of promise of marriage, unless he preferred fulfilling his promises.

The defendant could not deny his engagements with the plaintiff, because the pledges he had given her were produced in evidence against him; but he acknowledged having left her, on pretence that she was not of temperate habits, and offered on the previous Saturday, when the case was brought forward, to establish that fact by unquestionable evidence. The witnesses were this day examined on oath; and their testimony went to prove, that during the last review on l'Ancresse Common, and during the Whitsuntide holidays, when Jane Allet was in company with her betrothed, he had given her "some milk punch and some wine to drink, which had made her a little merry;" – her witnesses, however, declared that they had known her for many years, and they always looked upon her as a young woman of sober habits.

The Court, after hearing Advocate MACCULLOCH for the defendant, and the ATTORNEY-GENERAL for the plaintiff, were of opinion that NICHOLAS LE PAGE had failed to establish the charge he had preferred against JANE ALLET, and therefore condemned him to pay her the sum of £20, and costs.

The Comet, Vol XIV No 41, August 9 1841

Note: £20 would have been about half the average yearly income

Shocking Case

Not many days since, an elderly female, residing in Alderney, named DAVID, went into a field at a place called La Vallée, for the purpose of gathering nettles, when she was attacked by a boar, which bit her in the calf of one of her legs. The animal so lacerated the limb that a considerable haemorrhage took place. The poor woman cried out for help, and presently a man came to the spot, who on seeing her in that dreadful situation, immediately repaired to town, for medical assistance, but before the medical gentleman reached the place, the unfortunate woman had breathed her last.

The Comet, Vol VI No 30, July 12 1833

Plate 8: The Braye, Alderney

Elopement in High Life!

On Saturday morning last, an English gentlemen residing in this island, and who has a wife and nine interesting children, eloped with a young lady, aged about 23 years, the daughter of an English lady of high respectability, also a resident in this town. The guilty pair embarked on board her Majesty's packet Dasher, Captain WHITE, for Weymouth. We suppress the names of the fugitives, not wishing to add to the affliction of two respectable families, who are plunged into the depth of distress by such an unexpected and very painful affair.

The Comet, Vol XIV No 9, April 19 1841

The brig Charlotte, belonging to Mr. JOHN BONAMY, has been hauled upon the south Beach, for the purpose of being lengthened by Mr. T. DE LA MARE; and the cutter Julia, belonging to Mr. RICHARD SMALL, is to undergo the same operation by Mr. WILLIAM JONES, in the same locality. To say nothing of the risk which must, more or less, attend those enterprises during spring-tides, should it come to blow strong, the beach is at all times an uncomfortable place for men to work upon; but there is no alternative, so long as accommodations are withheld from enterprising shipbuilders and others. Good docks might be constructed here, if Guernseymen were awake to their own interests. But they are not!

The Comet, Vol XIV No 15, May 10 1841

Sudden Death

On Thursday afternoon last, whilst Mrs Elizabeth Foote, mother-in-law to Mr George Foote, was drinking tea in her usual health and spirits, she suddenly fell from her chair on the floor and expired, without uttering a sigh or groan! Medical aid was instantly procured, but it was to no avail, as the vital spark had left its tenement of clay. The deceased was in the 71st year of her age.

The Comet, Vol XII No 57, October 7 1839

A man, named JAMES PRITCHARD, a native of Hereford-shire, who had been sent to the Town Hospital, in consequence of an inflammation in his right foot, occasioned by wearing a tight boot, underwent amputation of that limb, below the knee, on Monday last, by Mr. CAREY, the Surgeon of that asylum. The operation was performed in a very adroit manner; and the poor man submitted to it with heroic courage. We are glad to say, that PRITCHARD is doing well.

The Comet, Vol XV No 104, March 16 1843

3

Island News and Customs

Yesterday, the poor of the Town Hospital were treated with ormers for dinner. We understand that 1704 of these shell fish were set before them, which they presently consumed with great satisfaction.

The Comet, Vol 1 No 46, February 9 1829

No part of the island is more subject at present to one disease than another, if we except hernias, which may be said to be more frequent in the lower parishes, where the granite quarries are worked.

The History of Guernsey, 1841
Jonathan Duncan

In Guernsey, when a young man offers himself to a young lady, and is accepted, the parents of the parties give what is termed a flouncing; that is, they invite their friends to a feast. The young lady is led round the room by her future father-in-law, and introduced to his friends, and afterwards the young man is paraded in like manner by his future father-in-law; then there is an exchange of rings and some articles of plate, according to the rank of the parties. After this, it is horrid for the damsel to be seen walking with any other male person, and the youth must scarce glance at anything feminine; in this way they court for years. After this ceremony, if the gentleman alters his mind, the lady can claim half his property; and if the fickle lass should repent, the gentleman can demand the half of hers.

Observations on Popular Antiquities, 1849
John Brand

Plate 9: Scene Looking South from Delancey

The Royal Artillery Militia, on Monday last, practised ball-firing in Belgreve Bay. A boat, with a target erected in it, was moored at about 600 yards distance from the shore, and upon that object the men of that corps exercised their skill. – The practice was good. There were sixteen field-pieces furnished with eight rounds each; thirty-six shot perforated the target; and in closing the exercises of that day, a general volley was discharged, – the boat was struck, and sunk to the bottom. The Guernsey Artillery had not, in our recollection, been exercised in this way before.

The Comet, Vol VI No 26, June 28 1833

We feel much pleasure in stating that the Guernsey Gaol contains only three prisoners; one debtor, one smuggler, and one criminal; while that of Jersey contains thirty-six criminals and sixteen debtors.

The Chit Chat, No 3, Vol 1, Guernsey, October 21 1837

On Friday last, at a meeting of the Committee of the Church Sunday School, it was decided to commence a Branch Sunday School in connection with St. John's Church, at the Amballes. We understand there are nearly one hundred children in that neighbourhood who are without any Sunday School instruction whatever!

The Comet, Vol X No 97, February 19 1838

Why is the Royal Court like an optician? Do you give it up? Because it make spectacles.

The Comet, Vol X No 79, December 25 1837

Plate 10: Royal Court-house

An epidemic disorder among that most useful class of animals – the horse, rages fearfully throughout this island. Numbers have died within a few weeks, and we are confidently informed that the veterinary surgeon who was sent for at the request of the States, has, at present, no less than three hundred under his care!

The Star, Vol XIV No 9, August 22 1826

Cricket

Gentlemen desirous of encouraging this manly game are requested to attend on the New Ground, at one o'clock precisely, on Wednesday next, for the purpose of forming a Club for the ensuing season.

The Comet, Vol XIX No 15, May 4 1848

The walls of our town are studded with posting-bills, announcing that a wrestling match, for money, is to come off in a field near Amherst in the course of next month. The bills pretend that this inhuman sport is to take place "by permission": but by whose authority it has been sanctioned, we are not told. The Royal arms and initials on the bill, we presume, are a forgery. Not very long since certain boxers arrived here from Jersey, for the purpose of having a fight; and no sooner were the constables apprized of the fact, than they prevented it, and the parties went about their business without accomplishing their object. The constables were perfectly right in preventing the pugilists from boxing and bruising each other; and, we ask, who has given "permission" to these wrestlers to pursue their savagery and kick each other's shins to pieces? Public feeling is shocked at the consideration that such disgraceful proceedings are tolerated in a christian country, their tendency being to brutalise the mind of those who participate in them. Wrestling is one of those gross acts of cruelty which ought not even to be named among those who make the least pretence to humanity. We are sure it would redound the honour of the country, that such "permission," if ever granted, were withdrawn, and the parties prevented from exhibiting their brutal spectacle.

The Comet, Vol XXII No 41, July 30 1849

If ever a class of men were entitled to our pity, it is those now stationed at Castle Cornet, when they have to be brought over to parade on the New Ground. Last Friday, they had to perform that service; and, it will be recollected, that on that day the wind was blowing fresh from the north east, piercingly cold, with occasional showers of rain. The hour fixed for parading was eleven o'clock; and at about half past eight, the first boatload left Castle Cornet, with the Highlanders, who, after landing at Deschamp's Causeway, were marched up to the entrance of Truchot Street where they had to wait till the last boatload arrived, which was after eleven o'clock – so that upwards of three hours were consumed in performing this service! The men of the 23d, however, did not seem to relish this boating concern; and, at low water, they crossed over the neck of the castle to the pier, nearly mid-leg deep in water; and then walked to the New Ground, to perform the duties assigned to them, wet as they were! The same individuals did not embark at the causeway till nearly two o'clock in the afternoon; and how long they were in crossing over in a boat to the Castle Cornet, we cannot say; but we know, that the last boatload did not reach the shore till three o'clock in the afternoon! However unpleasant such a service may be, when compared to what they had to do at the Isle of Wight, we presume they would more gladly submit to it, than to be engaged at the point of the bayonet in quelling riots among the inhabitants. We congratulate these brave fellows, that they have already encountered the most formidable part of their duties; and that, when they return to more comfortable quarters than they now occupy, they will not have to complain that they were called upon to contend against riotous or rebellious subjects in the island of Guernsey.

The Comet, Vol XVIII No 23, June 3 1844

Pedestrians have often complained of the irregularity with which persons walk our streets, at night; and owing to which, frequent collisions between individuals take place, which are not of the most pleasant character. This is particularly the case on Sabbath evenings, when people return from public worship. It so happens, that service ends much at the same time in the churches and chapels situated in the lower and in the upper parts of the town; so that the respective congregations meet each other full-butt, in ascending and descending the streets, whereby much confusion is created – especially in dark nights, and in rainy weather, when there are many umbrellas open. All this confusion might be avoided, and walking might be rendered more pleasant, safe and comfortable, if persons would avoid crossing the lines of their neighbours, as is too frequently the case. For instance, if persons who are going down High-street would keep the houses on their right, and if those who ascend the street would observe the same rule on the other side, everything would be orderly; and no man or woman would run foul of each other, to their mutual inconvenience. A little attention to this simple rule, would soon correct the evil complained of; and at once render walking pleasant and safe, instead of what it is now – disagreeable and dangerous.

The Comet, Vol XV No 52, September 15 1842

The children connected with both the hospitals, who have the benefit of good schools for both males and females, and who are decently clothed and well fed, are occasionally to be seen walking in the country with their attendant matrons and masters; and it is lamentable to observe the idiocy and distortion of features that are stamped on the majority of their countenances. This we believe to be attributable to the habit prevailing amongst the humbler classes of intermarriage among them between persons of too near a degree of consanguinity.

The Channel Islands, a Guide
Frank Fether Dally, 1860

A strange peculiarity amongst the natives of this island is their morbid taste for funerals. Not satisfied with numerous relatives, whose name is "legion," those of the humblest sphere swell the line of followers to the grave to the utmost possible extent; and the result is that these cavalcades, with their straggling and unconcerned attendants, who may be frequently met chatting and joking on their solemn errand, rob the ceremony of all its mournful and befitting attributes. Among the higher classes the same infatuation prevails, and needlessly-expensive funerals are ranked among the follies of the day, as involving many a family in inconvenient and excessive outlay.

The Channel Islands, a Guide
Frank Fether Dally, 1860

Plate 11: St Peters Port, from Castle Cornet

Notwithstanding the capaciousness of our splendid fish-market, on Saturday last, such was the supply of fish of almost every description of that which is found on our coast, that there was not a sufficient number of stalls to accommodate those persons who came there for the purpose of selling their fish. Of shell fish, turbot, and mackerel, there was an abundant supply, and in the evening nearly the whole had been sold off.

The Comet, Vol IX No 10, June 20 1836

There was a plentiful supply of fish in our Market, of every description, on Saturday last. The conger was very abundant. One boat's crew alone, caught between 800 and 900lbs weight; and the same crew, the week before last, caught in one night as many conger has weight together, 1900lbs.

The Comet, Vol IX No 43, August 22 1836

The Town Clock is about a quarter of an hour too fast.

The Comet, Vol VI No 98, March 7 1834

This being May-day the chimney-sweepers in this place had recourse to their diversions and sports in order to keep up the remembrance of former times. The sooty tribe appeared about the streets in dresses of the most fanciful description, and danced and capered about with all the buffoonery of merry-andrews. They appeared with the implements of their dusty trade, and gathered as many pence and half-pence, in a shovel, as they could collect from the inhabitants.

The Comet, Vol VII No 10, May 2 1834

Note: A "Merry Andrew" is a clown or buffoon

Extraordinary Dispatch!

On Tuesday last, a tradesman in this town, sent off an order for goods to Birmingham, by the Weymouth packet, and on Saturday morning he received, by the Lady De Saumarez, steamer, the goods which he had ordered on the preceding Tuesday, so that only four days intervened between the giving of the order, and receiving the goods ordered. What would our forefathers have said to this?

The Comet, Vol X No 7, April 17 1837

Plate 12: St Peter Port (Town Church)

The Meetings of the States are something like Angels' visits – few and far between, and therefore we are glad to hear that that Body will be convened on an early day, for the dispatch of important business.

The Comet, Vol XI No 94, February 14 1839

There has not been sufficient time to ascertain the state of public feeling respecting illuminations on the day of her MAJESTY'S nuptials, in England, but we learn from the London papers received this day, that several towns did not illuminate, having adopted the course pursued in Guernsey, - namely, supplying the poor with bread and meat.

The Comet, Vol XII No 94, February 13 1840

We would advise a certain would-be intelligent young woman, residing within one hundred miles of Hauteville, to leave off cutting such a dash as she does, also not to be so fond of giving parties, to entice young men from their duty; she will not get a lover a moment sooner for soaring so far above her rank and station in life; a humble young tradesman is dazzled by the splendour of her dress, and a gentleman doest not think her good enough for him. We suppress her name hoping that she will take a friend's advice.

The Chit Chat, No 72, February 16 1839

It is quite fashionable now for the cart to drag the horse, or, as the old saying has it, that the hens crow before the cocks. This is fully exemplified by certain young ladies of this town who are constantly roaming after their lovers.

The Chit Chat, No 78, March 30 1839

Plate 13

We would recommend a certain handsome gentleman, well acquainted with the Greffiers Office in Alderney, to take a pocket handkerchief to chapel, as to rub his long nose, and also blow it with his fingers, is very ungentlemanlike.

The Chit Chat, No 79, April 6 1839

Mysterious

A corpse, we understand, was found on Friday last in one of the hollows on the south side of the island of Alderney. The body, our informant states, has been identified as that of a man, a mason by trade, who suddenly disappeared in the month of November last. Its discovery was purely fortuitous, no one expecting to find the remains of the missing individual under such circumstances. Other particulars we have not been able to learn ; few persons seeming disposed to trouble themselves about such matters, and even less inclined to transmit them to be chronicled by the press of this island. Had such an event occurred in Australia, we would doubtless have heard of it in a direct way ; but as it happened at Alderney, which is almost at our own doors, it is more difficult to acquire information on the subject.

The Comet, Vol XXVII No 17, April 27 1854

4

Weather

On Thursday last, about 7 o'clock, in the evening, this island was visited by a dreadful storm of thunder and lightening, which lasted till after 10 o'clock at night. The lightening, in point of vividness, surpassed everything of the kind we had witnessed for many years past. At intervals the rain fell in copious and fertilising showers, to refresh the thirsty earth. No damage, we believe, has been sustained in any part of the island.

The Comet, Vol VIII No 47, September 7 1835

Yesterday was a complete winter's day. Early in the morning heavy showers of hail and snow fell over the island, and though the weather occasionally broke up at intervals, at noon the snow fell in immensely large flakes, such as we do not remember to have seen for many years past. Everything around bore the cheerless aspect of winter, and the weather was as cold as it frequently is in December, in our climate.

The Comet, Vol X1 No 31, July 8 1839

Note: The date of this edition of *The Comet* is correct!

On Saturday last, at about four o'clock in the afternoon, we had thunder and lightning, accompanied by one of the heaviest showers of hail we ever recollect to have seen, which lasted for some time. It was well that it occurred so late in the day, or our fair country women who statedly sell fruits and vegetables in our unsheltered market, would have had a pretty time of it, whilst the hail poured down in torrents. We do most sincerely hope that before many months have elapsed, the pity and compassion of the "lords of creation" in this part of the world will be so mollified as to lead them, in good earnest, to do something to remove the disgrace of our island – the absolute want of a sheltered Vegetable Market. If the merciful man feels compassion for the "life of his beast," surely merciful men should manifest infinitely more of that godlike disposition, for the comfort, convenience and health of his equals, and therefore we trust that this matter will be steadily kept in view and followed up, until this grand desideratum has been fully accomplished.

The Comet, Vol IX No 56, October 10 1836

During the last five weeks, the weather has been excessively wet, cold, and stormy at intervals, more resembling autumn than summer; but the last forty eight hours have been the finest we have had during that time. The wind is now easterly, with every appearance of settled weather. Let us pray for its continuance, in order that the fruits of the earth may be matured and brought to perfection, and that the poor of the land may eat cheap bread in abundance.

The Comet, Vol XIV No 25, June 12 1843

Plate 14: Town of St Peter Port, Guernsey

Thunderstorm

At about three o'clock yesterday afternoon, a thunder storm gathered over the eastern coast of this island, and proceeded in a NNE direction. It was of so sudden a nature and short duration, accompanied by such very large drops of rain and hailstones as to merit noticing. The morning had been fine, calm, and warm light mists floated occasionally over the blue ether; but at the time above mentioned a dark cloud was observed, rapidly increasing in size and density, in the SSW. The wind freshening wafted the surcharging element town-wards, when an out-pouring commenced. Its burden however was not to remain here; but continuing and accumulating in its course, reached the Vale and St Sampson's parishes. While it veiled over and shadowed the land, all for a moment was calm and silent; earth as if waiting in breathless suspense the issue of pent-up and raging elements above. The clouds, as it were unable to contain them longer, suddenly burst asunder, and large drops of rain, followed by hailstones between three and four inches in circumference, came pelting and hissing to the ground. Vivid lightning flashed and zig-zagged across the clouds' dark centre, and thunders rolled and re-echoed among the bays and neighbouring islands. This scene, though it lasted scarcely more than ten minutes, was truly grand and awful. All soon cleared up again, and the sun peeped forth from beneath his dark covert smiling at Old Jove thundering in the north. The thermometer now detected a sensible diminution of temperature, which has continued ever since. – The barometer falling, wind blowing fresh, southerly, seemingly portending rain, &c. &c. Had the hailstones fallen over the town, as they did further northward, our islanders' conservatories would have suffered considerable damage.

The Comet, Vol X11No 57, October 7 1839

Last Friday at seven o'clock in the evening there felt a smart shower of hail, some of the hail stones were quite as large as hazel nuts. It was preceded and attended by several vivid flashes of thunder, accompanied with heavy showers of rain.

The same day in the afternoon, a cart and horse, belonging to Mr John Brouard Jun. fell over the Quay into the Harbour, when there was no water in it. In the fall, one of the shafts got entangled among the ropes by which one of the vessels laying alongside the Quay was fastened, and the other rested against the side of the vessel, whereby the animal remained suspended, and after struggling for a little while, it got completely rid of its harness and fell to the ground, apparently without injury.

The Comet, Vol 1 No 6, May 5 1828

5

Crime and Punishment

Complaints have been made to us, that there are several persons who are in the habit of perambulating the town at unseasonable hours, who during their nightly rambles, amuse themselves with rapping at the doors of the peaceable inhabitants, whereby they are greatly annoyed by such unwelcome visits. In the course of last week, several persons of New Town, got out of their beds between two and three o clock in the morning to ascertain the cause of the violent knocking at their doors, but as soon as the disturbers of the public peace hear the least moving above stairs, scampered off with the utmost speed. We hope that those who have sufficient physical strength and courage will not fail, upon repetition of a similar offence, to endeavour to lay hold of such street walkers, and place them under the care of the police.

The Comet, Vol IV No 4, April 21 1828

An unloving and cruel husband

Abraham Torode, formerly a mariner, was placed at the bar of the court on Friday, for having on the preceding Wednesday, most unmercifully bitten his wife's nose, and lacerated it in a shocking manner. The deed was committed under circumstances of deep aggravation, for it was done at a time when, according to the outward act, he was, it was presumed, going to show his affection to his wife; but instead of kissing her as he pretended, he inflicted a wound whereby she is likely to be disfigured for the remainder of her life, to the disgrace of him who is the cause of it. The court condemned the offender to one month's solitary confinement in the public jail, the last fortnight to be on bread and water ...

The Comet, Vol III No 39, December 20 1830

... Desperate Suicide

On Wednesday last, a little before mid-day, A. Torode who so recently injured his wife, shot himself in the house in the lane leading to the Petites Fontaines, in the Town parish....

The Comet, Vol III No 47, February 14 1831

Note: The rest of this report is too gruesome to relate in this book!

Plate 15: St Pierre Port, Guernsey

Last Saturday, a miserable catch-penny was circulated about the streets of this town, in the shape of a handbill, purporting that a vessel which had sailed from Bristol for some undefined port, with upwards of 400 persons on board had been lost, and that "400 souls had perished," which turns out to be a wicked falsehood hatched up by some vile miscreant, for the purpose of making a penny at the expense of outraging public feeling. We wonder that such an act has been allowed to pass unnoticed by our authorities. It is shocking, that men for the sake of gain, are allowed to deal in such unhallowed stories, without being subjected to some heavy penalty.

The Comet, Vol IX No 59, October 20 1836

Note: 'catch penny' - any temporary contrivance to raise a contribution on the public. Definition taken from The 1811 *Dictionary of the Vulgar Tongue*, originally by Francis Grose.

Caged!

Mr Nicholas Le Page who on Saturday sennight was condemned by the Royal Court to be exposed in the cage in the public market, for having insulted and maltreated Mary-Ann Lane and Elizabeth Chidley, underwent that part of his sentence on Saturday last, from eleven till one o clock. The prisoner made nothing of it, and appeared perfectly indifferent to the gaze of some hundreds of spectators.

The Comet, Vol V No 3, April 9 1832

Accident

About five o'clock on Saturday evening last, a most melancholy event occurred to Charles McCarthy, a Porter, who was passing along the quay with a bag of coals upon his back; a cart suddenly backed upon him and there being no safeguard on the edge of the quay, he was precipitated into the harbour a fall of about 20 feet; he was taken up in a state of insensibility. The spectators acted with great humanity, and in a very short time several professional gentlemen were in attendance, but the sufferer was in such a condition that it was found necessary, without loss of time, to have him removed to the hospital, where he received that assistance which his case required, but up to last evening he remained perfectly insensible.

The Comet, Vol V No 16, May 25 1832

On Tuesday an investigation took place at the Royal Court touching the death of Charles McCarthy on Sunday last, who, on the preceding Saturday was precipitated into the harbour by a cart backing on him. It appeared that the driver, John Martel, son of John Martel of the Pavé, Câtel parish, was to blame, and the Court, having taken the evidence of witnesses held him to bail in the sum of £100 to take his trial whenever the Crown Lawyers shall instigate the same.

The Comet, Vol V No 16, May 25 1832

Plate 16: View from Clifton, Guernsey

John Martel, the carter, who in backing his cart on the Quay, on Saturday the 19th ult., precipitated Charles McCarthy into the harbour, so as to occasion his death on the following day, was tried on Saturday last before the Royal Court, at the suit of the Crown Lawyers. Several witnesses were heard on behalf of the prosecution, but it appeared that the accident was not occasioned by any misconduct or want of attention on the part of Martel, and therefore the Court acquitted him. Several witnesses gave the accused a most excellent character for sobriety, and being particularly attentive to his business.

The Comet, Vol V No 19, June 4 1832

In the course of last week some malicious individual daubed over with paint the front of several shops in High Street, some of which had been recently painted afresh. Such an act is one of mere wantonness, and it is to be regretted that the perpetrator is unknown. No possible motive can be assigned, but such as must flow from down right wickedness, for such abominable conduct. We hope the shopkeepers in High Street will use every exertion in their power to discover the author of such a disgraceful act.

The Comet, Vol VI No 15, May 20 1833

Three young men of St. Saviour's parish, named William Le Poidevin, Charles De Garis, and Henry Brehaut were brought to the bar of the Court on Saturday by the constable of that parish, accused of having insulted several young women and other persons who were returning one evening from St. Peter's chapel.

The Court sentenced them to a fortnight's solitary confinement in the public jail, on bread and water.

The Star, Vol XIII No 31, January 24 1826

We understand that during the last few days several unwelcome visits have been paid to the larders of different persons in the Town, and that the unexpected guests have made more free than welcome with the contents of these depositaries of desirable things – beef, ham &c. has been carried off by those uncalled for visitors, and therefore the inhabitants of St Peter Port will do well to be on the look-out, in order to prevent, and detect the depredations that may be meditated upon their eatables. Some of those depredations had been committed in the very heart of the town, and that certainly proves the audacity of those concerned in them.

The Comet, Vol VI No 4, August 16 1833

Plate 17: View from near the Cement Mills, St Saviours, Guernsey

Elizabeth Le Tocq was placed at the bar accused of keeping a house of ill-fame, and also of harbouring young girls belonging to the Town Hospital; she was found guilty, and sentenced to a fortnight's solitary confinement on bread and water. She is recommended to the care of the Overseers of the Poor.

The Comet, Vol VII No 26, June 26 1834

The knocker-breakers have resumed their nightly depredations. Only a few evenings since, between the hours of nine and ten, they wantonly wrenched off the knocker on one of Mr Wakely's houses, opposite the College, and then audaciously wrapped it up in a piece of paper and placed it on the step of the door, directed to the lady by whom the house is tenanted!

The Comet, Vol VII No 92, February 13 1835

Francoise Archenaux, who on Saturday sennight was convicted by the Royal Court of having attempted to poison the family of Mr Daniel Grut Le Masurier, under went a part of her sentence by being placed in the cage in the public market from half-past eleven to half-past twelve. On the four squares of the cage was fastened a printed label signifying the crime for which she was punished, it read thus, namely "Empoisonneuse". There was a multitude of both sexes present to witness the exhibition, whom she addressed at some length, but of the purport of her harangue we know nothing.

The Comet, Vol VII No 63, November 3 1834

On Saturday last, FRANCOISE ARCHENAUX, the French young woman, who about three months since was convicted of having attempted to administer rat poison mixed up in a bottle of white wine to the family of MR DANIEL LE MASURIER, was exhibited for the second time in the cage in the market-place, from half past ten in the morning to half past twelve at noon, pursuant to her sentence. She harangued the by-standers at intervals during her exhibition. Her solitary confinement on bread and water for three months, seems to have weakened her constitution, for she appeared to walk back to jail with some difficulty.

The Comet, Vol VII No 87, January 26 1835

On Saturday last, MARY TOSDEVIN, a native of the Catel parish, was committed for trial, on a charge of having concealed her pregnancy of an illegitimate child, of which she was delivered on the 2nd of September instant, and for not having prepared baby-linen for its reception on its coming into the world. She pleaded guilty; but on account of the state of her health, she was not sent to jail, but is kept in the Hospital for the present. The child to which she had given birth was found on the 15th instant, in the cess-pool of a pig stye on Mr. Peter Le Page's estate, at the Ozouët, in this parish, with whom the accused lived in the capacity of servant.

The Comet, Vol IX No 51, September 19 1836

On Saturday last, Mary Tostevin was tried before the Royal Court, on the indictment of the CROWN LAWYERS, charging her with her having clandestinely been delivered of a male child on the 2nd of September last, in the house of her master, Mr. Peter Le Page at the Ozouëts, parish of St Peter Port; and also for concealing her pregnancy. The facts of this case being unfit for publication, we therefore suppress them. The prisoner having been found guilty, the Court condemned her to two month's imprisonment.

The Comet, Vol IX No 69, November 21 1837

On Saturday last, ELIZABETH BRENAM, who had been convicted of theft in the house of JOHN S. BROCK, Esq., and also in that of Mr. J. THOMAS, Market-place, by the Royal Court, on the preceding Saturday, underwent the first part of her sentence, namely – exposure in the cage, in the Market-square, from eleven to twelve o'clock. The weather being very wet, there was not the usual concourse of spectators to witness such an exhibition. The prisoner will be transported forthwith, during a period of three years, from this bailiwick.

The Comet, Vol X No 79, December 25 1837

The following story affords a fine specimen of the rapaciousness of the Custom-house laws in France:- A few days ago, the John, Capt. MACHON, arrived at Perros, from this port, when the Douaniers went on board to examine the vessel as usual. They found that the knives and forks, tea cups and saucers, frying-pan, &c. &c., for the use of the cabin, were new; and because they had not yet been used, they seized and kept the whole of them, and left the captain without knife or fork, tea cup, or frying-pan, to make use of. Captain MACHON applied to the Inspector for redress, but it was utterly useless, – although he assured him that the articles were solely for the ship's use. All he could say had not the least effect with those cormorants of the law, as they retained possession of every article.

The Comet, Vol X No 103, March 19 1838

Melancholy Affair

On Saturday evening last, a man named JOHN BLYTH, by trade a biscuit baker, died from the effect of taking one ounce of laudanum, under the following distressing circumstances:

It appears that two days before he had drank a pint of cold water, which had brought on diarrhœ, and he complained to one of his fellow-workmen that he was very ill; the man advised him to take three-pence worth of the tincture of rhubarb, saying it would do him good. He took his advice, and sent a little boy named SEWARD to Mr. GARDNER'S, druggist, Country Mansell, for the quantity in question. Mr. GARDNER was in the shop with his apprentice, JAMES DE LA MARE, a young lad sixteen years of age, who has been six years at the business, and has been accustomed to dispense medicine. The master, who was busy at his desk at the time, allowed his apprentice to give the article required. In taking down a bottle from the shelf he thought he had that containing the tincture of rhubarb, and measured out an ounce and gave it to the boy; but when he came to replace the bottle, he perceived, by the label upon it, that he had given laudanum instead of rhubarb! He immediately informed Mr. GARDNER of the mistake, who, knowing what the consequence would be to BLYTH if he swallowed the drug, ran out instantly, and went to the bake-house where the deceased used to work, with the view to prevent him taking the laudanum; but when he arrived there he found it was too late, as BLYTH had drank the whole! He then told him to introduce his fingers down his throat in order to cause a discharge from the stomach, and then hastened back with all possible speed to his shop and procured an emetic, which he administered himself, which caused partial discharge of the contents of the stomach. But wishing to leave nothing undone in order to save the man's life, if possible, he went to Dr. TYNDALL, and requested him to attend; but the Doctor said he was engaged, and could not come. In the next place, Mr. GARDNER called on Mr. Bisson, but he was not at home, and finally he secured Mr. HEWER's services, who administered another emetic, but it produced no effect; and then he took from the deceased twelve or fourteen ounces of blood. Mr. HEWER remained with the deceased till about nine o'clock in the evening, when he appeared to be better; but shortly afterwards a re-action took, and at half-past ten o'clock, BLYTH expired!

The Court met in private this morning to investigate the affair. Several witnesses were examined, and at the close of examination the public were admitted to hear the verdict, which was – that BLYTH"s death had been caused by taking one ounce of laudanum, which had been sold to the boy SEWARD by mistake, for the tincture of rhubarb, without there having been the slightest intention to do him any harm.

It appeared that the deceased was addicted to the immoderate use of spirituous liquors, and that his frame was greatly emaciated in consequence of his intemperate habits, so that his constitution was not sufficiently vigorous to resist the effect of the poison which he had inadvertently taken.

The Comet, Vol X No 101, March 12 1838

Distressing affair – A Lady shot by her own servant!

Last evening, between the hours of seven and eight o'clock, Mrs Du Bour, a french lady, aged about seventy or eighty years, and mother of Mr Du Bour, was shot dead under the following melancholy circumstances. It appears that about six weeks ago, some articles had been stolen from the premises occupied by Mr Du Bour, at the Villocq, Catel parish, and therefore, in order to protect himself and property, ever since that period he has been in the habit of keeping loaded pistols in his house, which he kept in his private room.

Yesterday, being what is called in the Church of Rome, "Dimanche Gras", (or the Sunday before Lent,) a day which is kept up as a kind of Carnival by the members belonging to that communion, - and which seems to have been the case at Mr Du Bours ; between the hours of seven and eight o'clock in the evening, the inmates of the house, and others, were amusing themselves, as is customary on such occasions, when the French servant, named Nanette Posmier, who was dressed in her master's clothes, went into his apartment, where his pistols were kept; - she took up one of them, without knowing it was loaded with shot, and presenting it to her aged mistress, in sport, and pulled the trigger; - the load exploded, and the contents lodged in Mrs Du Bour's breast, which, in a few minutes after deprived her of her mortal, - thereby affording another affecting proof, to the thousands already upon record, of the injudiciousness of allowing loaded fire-arms to remain within the reach of children or domestics, who are too fond, in general, of amusing themselves with those instruments of death, under circumstances when they little apprehend any danger, as was the case in the present instance; inasmuch as this unfortunate servant was mostly sincerely attached to the deceased lady, but who, in an unsuspecting moment, turned the house of mirth into one of lamentation, weeping, and woe!

An investigation took place this morning at the Court House representing the cause respecting the cause of this melancholy affair, when sufficient evidence was adduced to satisfy the Court that this sad catastrophe was purely accidental.

The Comet, Vol XI No 94, February 14 1839

Eighteen boys were this day brought up before the Court of Correctional Police, being accused of having broken nearly all the windows in the house belonging to an old woman named BREHAUT, of St. Sampson's Parish, and also of having grossly insulted her, at different times. The young urchins were found guilty, and the Court condemned them to pay a fine of £3 to her Majesty. It appeared that the old woman had not been very sparing in the use of her tongue towards the boys, or, in all probability, the punishment would have been more severe.

The Comet, Vol XIII No 6, April 9 1840

On Monday night, some miscreant, in passing along Hauteville, threw a stone, as large as a man's fist through a window in the first floor of a LADY'S house, which struck her on the back whilst she was in bed! The missile must have been thrown with considerable force, for although the window-blind was drawn down, it did not arrest it in its course. Had the LADY been struck about the head, there is no knowing what might have been the consequence. We regret to record such a fact, because it proves the existence of a reckless disposition in some individual residing here, which we had hoped was not to be found in Guernsey.

The Comet, Vol XIII No 28, June 25 1840

This morning, MAURICE DE COURCY, Esq, was brought before the Court of Correctional Police, charged with an assault upon a boy named KNIGHT, by having (not in a very gentle manly manner), pulled one of his ears, and torn his shirt-collar. The charge having been fully proved, the Court fined Mr. DE COURCY seven livres tournois, (ten shillings), together with the expenses.

The Comet, Vol XIII No 68, November 12 1840

A young man, named PETER BEAN, was this day brought before the Court, accused of having, at four o'clock yesterday morning, climbed over the wall of the garden belonging to Misses MARTINEAU, at the Vale, and stolen therefrom sixteen flowers, their property. The prisoner was detected in the act by two men who had been placed to watch over the garden, by those ladies, in consequence of the frequent depredations of this sort of which they have been subjected from time to time. The Court, with the view to check, as far as possible, such pilferings, condemned the accused to one month's imprisonment, and to pay 16s. for the flowers.

The Comet, No XIV No 13, May 3 1841

Plate 18: The Terre and South Beach, Guernsey

Last Saturday, James Ledford, convicted of burglary, underwent the first part of his sentence, by being whipped, within the precincts of the jail-yard. The doors of the prison were thrown open to the public; and as many as could be accommodated with room availed themselves of the opportunity to witness the infliction of the punishment. Yesterday, Ledford went to Jersey, for the purpose of fetching his traps, - from whence, he says, he is going to his friends, to spend the Christmas holidays!

The Comet, Vol XV No 79, 19 December 1842

An act of singular barbarity was committed on Saturday last in the Bordage. Two horses belonging to country people were put into the stable of Mr. Le Page during the market hours, and some malicious person cut off their tails and left them bleeding. Have any steps been taken to discover the villains and bring them to justice?

The Star, Vol XIII No 42, April 11 1826

Highway Robbery!

Last Monday night, shortly after 9 o-clock, a young man named JAMES GREEN, (saddler), was stopped on the highway, near the DEPUTY SHERIFF's house, at the Ruette Brayes, by three men, all armed with sticks. One of the fellows came up to him, (the other two standing at a short distance), and, brandishing his stick over GREEN's head, ordered him to give up what money he had about his person, or he would lay him prostrate on the ground! In the meantime, the footpad took five francs from GREEN, and, before he went off, told him that if he would meet him near the burial grounds on Friday night, about seven or eight o'clock, he would return his money! One of the fellows wore a high glazed hat; another had on a tarpawling hat; the other, a southwester and canvass trowsers. From this description, it is probable that the villains were disguised in order to avoid detection, should they be met with in daytime.

The Comet, Vol XVIII No 72, November 21 1844

Plate 19: Petit Bo Bay, from behind the Mill

The Detective Force detected!

An incident occurred during the night of Friday last, so ludicrous in its character – yet so instructive – that, despite the fear of official displeasure, we cannot refrain giving it further publicity. It appears that between the hours of eleven and twelve on the above night, a lady residing at the Rohais was awoke from her slumbers by hearing a conversation beneath her windows. The lady rose, looked out, and observed three suspicious looking men in the road, who were whispering to each other. She listened attentively – she thought they were on no good errand – she saw them part – and, at parting, they were heard to say, "We shall meet at midnight"! What was to be done? The good lady – acting on the truism, that prevention is better than cure – succeeded in arousing her neighbours; and one of them (a young gentleman) was despatched to the town for the police, two of whom immediately rose, dressed themselves, and took to the road –

They searched above – they searched below – But nothing could they find!

At about one o'clock, however, the police fell in with the identical three; when it was discovered that, instead of robbers, they were men appointed by the police to try and discover midnight depredators! And the unfortunate constables returned home about two o'clock on Saturday morning – doubtless, not a little disconcerted by their adventure. The affair soon got bruited abroad – of course, with some little variations: the thieves being said to have been captured in an attempt to enter the town church; the belfry-door of which, not having been closed on the previous evening, was found open, -and during the day afforded a topic of mirth to those not concerned in the wild-goose chase. It was not a bad thought altogether, that, in the appointment of these watchers, it was, as it were, intended to sweep and light the town at the same time!

The Comet, Vol XVIII No 72, November 25 1844

Police Court – September 7

(before H. O. Carre, Esq., Lieutenant-Bailiff; with Edgar McCulloch and Alfred S. Collings, Esqrs., Jurats.)

Charlotte Hendy (21), Sarah Payton (21), Jane Cummings (21), Judith Pinchmin (24), Elizabeth Norton (21), Mary Ann Moles (about 22), Elizabeth Gregg (between 17 and 18), and Ellen Porter (18), who are all infamous characters, were charged with being public nuisances and the authors of nightly disorders in various parts of the town.

The four assistant-constables, who appeared as witnesses against the prisoners, stated that the police were occasioned more trouble by those eight women than by all the town united. They occupied a house belonging to John Sarre, in Rosemary Lane, - the St. Giles of our town, - and, when the police were presumed to have retired to their respective homes, these human owls were wont to issue from their retreat, and commit manifold offences against the public peace and public decency. Besides these general accusations, specific charges were brought against them. They were stated to have instigated, and taken part in, a disturbance at the "Buvette," a dram-shop, on the Quay on Saturday last. And on the Sunday morning, between 2 and 3 o'clock, Assistant-Constable Goubey was called to quell a disorder which took place in their den of infamy, in Rosemary Lane. An artilleryman had been thrown out of a window by four line soldiers, and had received certain injuries on the head by his fall. The interior of this resort presented a spectacle which decorum forbids us to describe. At the rear of the house is a garden or yard, and the scenes and sounds of debauchery and riot in the Pandemonium had obliged the disgusted neighbours to darken their windows with whitewash, and determine to quit the vicinage altogether. There is more in our town than the philosophy of many of its quiet inhabitants recks of. Our matter-of-fact police, however, appear to

"- Forget how superior, for mortals below,
Is the fiction them dream to the truth that they know." *

They have sacked a nest of misery and vice, and our only regret is that the act has not been still more effectual.

The Court condemned the eight abandoned creatures to fifteen days' imprisonment each, the first and the last five in solitary confinement and on bread and water. Hendy and Payton, who have no legal domicile in this island, were further sentenced to give bail, in the sum of £5 each, for their future good conduct during three months, or, in default, to quit the island. This is equivalent to banishment, to which, it is unfortunate, all their companions could not be condemned.

The Comet, September 1849

* From the poem by Thomas Hood 'To the Invisible Girl'.

Complaints are loud and deep respecting the prevalence of juvenile delinquency and crime. The subject everywhere attracts attention on account of the fearful aspect which it bears upon the future condition of society, as well as upon the ultimate destiny of the individuals involved. The evil is deplored; but the great problem to be solved is, what kind of remedy will be most effectual to the extermination, or, at least, to the subjugation of vice, and, in the meantime, be the means of rescuing its unhappy subjects from shame and infamy? Various methods, under diversified circumstances, have been tried with very little effect; and we fear that no permanently corrective result will follow where punitive measures alone are adopted. These should be seconded by moral and religious instruction by competent individuals.

As such instruction is not found in connexion with the mode of punishment inflicted upon offenders in Guernsey, to look for any moral reformation is very much akin to an expectation of reaping fruit without sowing seed. We grant that a luxuriant crop of thorns and other noxious productions may be expected. If proof of the correctness of our views on the foregoing melancholy topic were required, a mere glance at the markets would suffice – abundant evidence being there furnished. What do you behold therein? A gang of wretched boys trained up in the sheerest idleness – that nurse of crime – depending upon the precarious means which the occasional carrying of a basket of provisions afford; persons who engage the services of those boys incurring the risk of being despoiled by a portion of the articles entrusted to their care. And when the degraded urchins have realised a few pence in this way – and at other times by means less honourable – instead of giving their earnings to their parents, they waste them in card-playing, and drinking at low public-houses. They there put a finishing stroke to their depravity by contracting vicious habits, which totally unfit them for the commendable pursuits of society. Their very employment tends to demoralise their principles. It is therefore questionable whether they should be so employed.

The evil complained of is so glaring and palpable, that the subject, we understand, will soon be formally brought under the notice of the civil authorities. The idlers in question infest the markets not only in day-time, but at night, when they congregate in groups, and, by their vociferations and horrid imprecations become an intolerable nuisance to the neighbourhood, as well as to those whom business leads in that direction. We bring these facts before the public, because they are of such character as should not admit toleration in a well-regulated society. We do sincerely hope that those whom it more particularly concerns to watch over the morals of youth will devise some efficacious plan to check an evil which contains the germ of those crimes which result from the uncontrolled exercise of the worst passions of a depraved nature.

The Comet, Vol XXI No 77, December 14 1848

Plate 20: Market Horses, St Peter Port, Guernsey

Police Court

John Ward, conductor of the omnibus called the Favourite, was produced by Mr. Webb, accused of having wickedly driven the pole of his omnibus into the door of the omnibus called the Albert, belonging to Mr. Pike; and also for having driven his vehicle so close to the Albert as to prevent passengers from getting into that vehicle. The Court found him guilty, and condemned him to three days' solitary confinement on bread and water; and reserved to Mr. Pike his right of action against the proprietor of the Favourite, for the payment of the damage above alluded to.

The Comet, Vol XVI No 56, September 28 1843

6

Demon Drink

Dreadful Effects of Drunkenness

On Monday last, a Mrs. Dumaresq, who lived in one of the houses in Commercial Arcade, was found dead in her room, by some of the lodgers residing under the same roof. It appears that this woman was addicted to the practice of drinking spirituous liquors immoderately, and when discovered to be a corpse, there was a bottle containing ardent spirits laying at her side! The mind recoils with instinctive horror at the relation of such an astounding fact, and one cannot but lament that those frequent occurrences have so little practical influence upon those person who are addicted to such beastly practices. One would suppose that awful cases of this description would operate as a salutary warning to drunkards in general, to beware of their sottish habits, by reminding them that the same causes, in many instances, produce the same effects, and that they have every thing to dread if they continue in the pursuit of such destructive courses. But there is reason to fear that the state of habitual drunkards is almost a hopeless one, as they seem to be proof against every remedy proposed for their recovery from the bodily and mental degradation into which they have voluntarily plunged themselves, by their unaccountable attachment to their intoxicating cups; and we are of opinion that there is no vice to which human nature is addicted, so difficult to be eradicated, as that under consideration; so that when one of these persons is induced to break off his debasing habits and becomes a thoroughly sober man, it may truly be said that a "legion" of other vices were driven out of him at the same time. Few there are of this description, it is true; nevertheless, every attempt should be perseveringly made to bring such deluded persons to a better mind, in order that they may be reclaimed, if possible, from a condition which cannot be viewed with the deepest commiseration, by every genuine philanthropist.

The Comet, Vol IX No 68, November 17 1836

Fatal Effects of Intemperance

Saturday evening, several persons met together in the parish of St Andrew's to partake of a supper which had been prepared consequent on the finishing of a new house which had been erected in that parish. They kept it up till a late hour in feasting to excess, and one of the party named John Le Page, a Blacksmith residing at St Martin, got so inebriated, that instead of returning home, he slept in the house with three other individuals, and awful to relate, in the morning, when his companions awoke, they found Le Page a corpse! We understand, the unfortunate man has left a wife and large family to deplore his untimely end.

The Comet, Vol I No 6, May 5 1828

Plate 21: Rocque du Guet, Cobo Bay

Mr Joseph Perry publican, late of Fountain Street, who on account of his improper behaviour had been sent away from the island, shortly after his arrival at The Bear Inn, Weymouth, while in a state of mental derangement, he threw himself out of the third story on the pavement in the street, by which his neck was broken and he died a few minutes after the fall.

The Comet, Vol IV No 4, April 21 1828

The debtors in our prison, whose beverage is restricted to half a bottle of wine per day, with as much small beer as they like to drink, applied to the Court on Saturday for the indulgence of having bottled-ale added thereto. The Court took the subject into consideration, and, after due reflection, refused to grant it; they, however, left it optional with the applicants to have bottled-ale instead of wine, but they would not allow both. Surely, when a man in those circumstances is allowed half a bottle of wine per day, together with small beer to his heart's ease, he ought to be satisfied with such allowance.

The Comet, Vol XIII No 53, September 21 1840

This day sennight a man named JOHN KITTS was found in a stone quarry at the Charotterie, in a state of complete insensibility. The men by whom he was discovered, very humanely carried him at the steam-mill belonging to Messrs. GUERIN BROTHERS, and placed him over the boiler, in hope that the heat might restore animation, as the man appeared to be lifeless. This being done, Dr. CHURCHILL was sent for, and after examining the man, he found his case to be of urgent necessity, and sent notice to that effect to Mr. THOMAS MAUGER, the Master of the Town Hospital, who admitted KITTS under those circumstances. Dr. W. MONK, parish surgeon, was immediately sent for, and when he arrived the man appeared to be dead, as no pulse could be perceived. Dr. MONK instantly applied the stomach pump, and threw into the stomach about three pints of warm liquid, and afterwards ordered the patient to be put into a hot bath, the temperature of which was 100 degrees. Friction was subsequently resorted to, and warm flannels applied, and in about two hours Mr. Monk had the pleasing satisfaction of seeing his efforts crowned with complete success, and Kitts may in truth say that he has been brought from the margin of the grave. Should this article meet his eye, we hope he will seriously reflect upon his narrow escape from the jaws of death, and avoid the beastly practice which placed him in those alarming circumstances.

The Comet, Vol IX No 100, March 9 1837

7

Weird and Wonderful

Novel Sighting

On Friday evening last, the Northern Lights so beautifully illuminated our hemisphere, that many of the inhabitants not adverting to the cause, imagined that some conflagration had taken place in some part of the Island, but after a little reflection, they discovered their error, and were highly gratified whilst gazing upon a sight so novel in this quarter of the globe.

The Comet, Vol III No 42, January 10 1831

Remarkable Phenomenon

On Friday night shortly after 10 o'clock, we witnessed a striking phenomenon in the heavens at about 10 or 12 degrees above the horizon. It appeared like a solid body of fire, and nearly as large as the sun at its rising. It kept on increasing and diminishing, and vice versa, for twenty minutes, when it disappeared from our view. Its situation was, as near as we can guess, in a S.S.E. direction from the Harbour :- above it the clouds were impenetrably dark, but below the object there was a clear sky down to the horizon which extended three or four miles in length, and formed a perfect contrast with the other part of the heavens.

The Comet, Vol IX No 98, March 2 1837

A few days ago, a wild Pigeon was shot by Mr Daniel Dorey, on his estate called the Gronez, in Câtel parish, and when the person who had the dressing of the bird, came to open it, she found in it's stomach thirteen acorns, which measured together fourteen inches and five eights in length.

The Comet, Vol IV No 35, November 21 1831

Marine Animal Sagacity

A few days ago a person residing in the Town parish, purchased in the fish market a large CRAB, and kept it alive in salt water during three days, and after that period, he took it down to the south beach and placed it on a bed of oysters. This marine animal had not been there long before it perceived an oyster opening its mouth, when the crab seized a stone with one of its claws and thrust it into the oyster's mouth, and with the other claw gutted the oyster as completely, and as cleanly, as could have been accomplished by the most adroit fisherman in Billingsgate Market.

The Comet, Vol VI No 52, September 27 1833

Plate 22: Moulin Huet Bay

An Immense Cabbage

There is now growing in a garden belonging to Mr D Gavet, Saint Saviour's parish, a cabbage of an extraordinary size. Its whole length from the surface of the ground to the top, measures sixteen feet in length, and is proportionably large! It is a curiosity, and may be seen at any time.

The Comet, Vol VII No 2, July 4 1834

Extraordinary Cabbages

About twelve months since, we stated that Mr Daniel GAVET, of the Croute, parish of Saint Saviour's had growing on his estate a cabbage which was then 16 or 17 feet in height. Since that period it has continued to grow still more, and it has now attained the extraordinary height of nineteen feet seven inches and a half!

It is now in blossom and fast hastening to seed. This wonderful production of nature is four years old. Mr Gavet will feel pleasure in supplying any person with seed, who may be desirous of obtaining it, on giving him a call any day of the week, Sundays excepted.

The Comet, Vol VIII No 22, June 12 1835

Remarkable Coincidence

On Thursday last, one of the boys belonging to the National School, named PETER MAHY, (of about eight years of age), son of PETER, while reading in one of the Bible Classes, all of a sudden dropped on the floor and remained in a state of insensibility for about twenty minutes afterwards. The Master of the School for sometime thought that life was extinct, as he could perceive neither respiration nor pulsation. The boy's mother was instantly sent for, who, on her arrival, was greatly alarmed at seeing her child in that state, but in about an hour after the boy was so far recovered as to be able to walk home with the assistance of his parent, and two of his school-mates; but what renders the affair remarkable is, that he had just finished reading the 31st verse of the xxii. Chapter of the Book of Numbers, couched in these terms: - "Then the Lord opened the eyes of Balaam, and he saw the Angel of the Lord standing the way, and his sword drawn in his hand; and he bowed his head and fell flat on his face."

The Comet, Vol IX No 76, December 19 1836

Plate 23: Pier Head, St Peter Port

Guernsey

On the afternoon of Dec. 29th, at a few minutes before four o'clock, the shock of an earthquake was felt throughout the whole of the island: the sky was partially overcast, and had a rainy appearance, the wind blowing in slight squalls from the southward and south-westward. At the time above mentioned, a loud rumbling, or undulating noise, was heard in every part of the island, accompanied by one or two shocks, which, the account states, had much less affinity to the concussion, produced by an explosion, than to the benumbing effect created by electricity. This phenomenon, it is generally agreed, lasted about four seconds, and was evidently subterranean. We learn from Sark that the shock was felt in that island at about the same time and in the same manner as in Guernsey.

The Yearbook of Facts in Science and Art
by John Timbs – 1844

On Wednesday last, about four o'clock in the afternoon, a water-spout fell in the neighbourhood of l'Ancresse Bay. At that moment, there happened to be a boat of about 10 feet keel, manned by two men, in the offing, with four sails set, which received the contents of the spout. The boat whirled round and round, and then capsized; when part of the ballast fell out, which prevented her from foundering, and she lay on her beam-ends on the surface of the water. As there were several fishermen in their boats in the bay at the time, they hastened to the rescue of the men, and took them into their boats. The boat which had been struck by the water spout, was subsequently righted, and towed on shore. At six o'clock in the evening, the remnant of the water spout expended itself in town, the rain having fallen with great impetuosity, resembling in some measure the rushing of a mighty wind.

The Comet, Vol XV No 37, July 25 1842

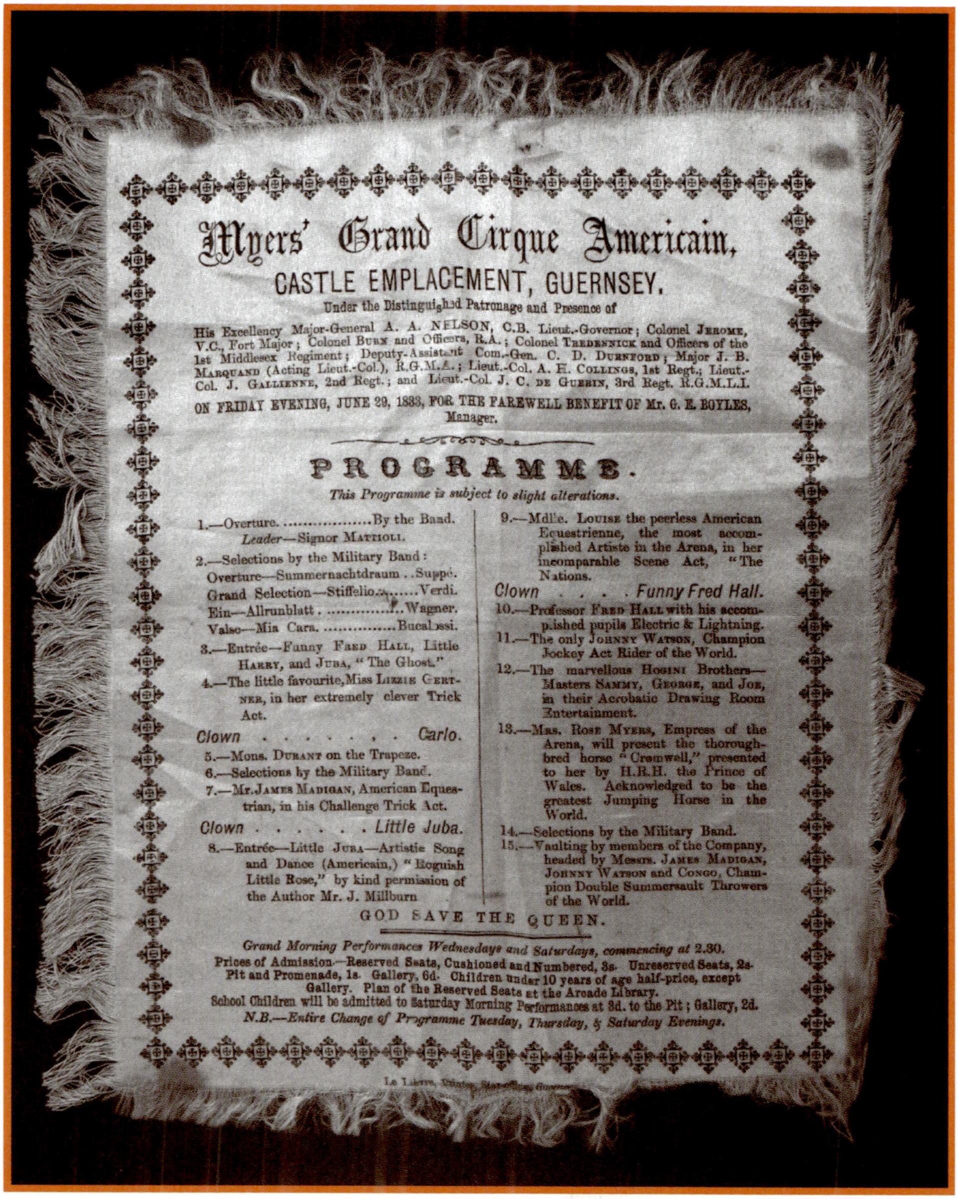

Myers' Grand Cirque Americain,

CASTLE EMPLACEMENT, GUERNSEY.

Under the Distinguished Patronage and Presence of

His Excellency Major-General A. A. NELSON, C.B. Lieut.-Governor; Colonel JEROME, V.C., Fort Major; Colonel BURN and Officers, R.A.; Colonel TREDENNICK and Officers of the 1st Middlesex Regiment; Deputy-Assistant Com.-Gen. C. D. DURNFORD; Major J. B. MARQUAND (Acting Lieut.-Col.), R.G.M.A.; Lieut.-Col. A. H. COLLINGS, 1st Regt.; Lieut.-Col. J. GALLIENNE, 2nd Regt.; and Lieut.-Col. J. C. DE GUERIN, 3rd Regt. R.G.M.L.I.

ON FRIDAY EVENING, JUNE 29, 1883, FOR THE FAREWELL BENEFIT OF Mr. G. E. BOYLES, Manager.

PROGRAMME.

This Programme is subject to slight alterations.

1.—Overture..................By the Band.
Leader—Signor MATTIOLI.

2.—Selections by the Military Band:
Overture—Summernachtdraum . . Suppé.
Grand Selection—Stiffelio..........Verdi.
Ein—Allrunblatt . ...Wagner.
Valse—Mia Cara. ....Bucalossi.

3.—Entrée—Funny FRED HALL, Little HARRY, and JUBA, "The Ghost."

4.—The little favourite, Miss LIZZIE GERTNER, in her extremely clever Trick Act.

Clown . . . . Carlo.

5.—Mons. DURANT on the Trapeze.

6.—Selections by the Military Band.

7.—Mr. JAMES MADIGAN, American Equestrian, in his Challenge Trick Act.

Clown . . . . Little Juba.

8.—Entrée—Little JUBA—Artistic Song and Dance (Americain,) "Roguish Little Rose," by kind permission of the Author Mr. J. Millburn

9.—Mdlle. LOUISE the peerless American Equestrienne, the most accomplished Artiste in the Arena, in her incomparable Scene Act, "The Nations.

Clown . . . . Funny Fred Hall.

10.—Professor FRED HALL with his accomplished pupils Electric & Lightning.

11.—The only JOHNNY WATSON, Champion Jockey Act Rider of the World.

12.—The marvellous HOGINI Brothers—Masters SAMMY, GEORGE, and JOE, in their Acrobatic Drawing Room Entertainment.

13.—MRS. ROSE MYERS, Empress of the Arena, will present the thorough-bred horse "Cromwell," presented to her by H.R.H. the Prince of Wales. Acknowledged to be the greatest Jumping Horse in the World.

14.—Selections by the Military Band.

15.—Vaulting by members of the Company, headed by Messrs. JAMES MADIGAN, JOHNNY WATSON and CONGO, Champion Double Summersault Throwers of the World.

GOD SAVE THE QUEEN.

Grand Morning Performances Wednesdays and Saturdays, commencing at 2.30.
Prices of Admission—Reserved Seats, Cushioned and Numbered, 3s. Unreserved Seats, 2s. Pit and Promenade, 1s. Gallery, 6d. Children under 10 years of age half-price, except Gallery. Plan of the Reserved Seats at the Arcade Library.
School Children will be admitted to Saturday Morning Performances at 3d. to the Pit; Gallery, 2d.
N.B.—Entire Change of Programme Tuesday, Thursday, & Saturday Evenings.

Plate 24

A few days ago, Mr. NELSON, one of the clowns of BATTY's Circus, made known to the public, that on Wednesday (yesterday) evening he would, like DIOGENEs, embark, in a tub, on the bosom of Old Neptune, which would be propelled through the water, from Castle Cornet to the harbour, by a given number of ducks! The announcement of this novel mode of water conveyance was enough to excite the utmost curiosity of the inhabitants; and, by five o'clock, some thousands of persons, of all ranks and conditions in society, were congregated on both piers, along the quays, on board and in the rigging of the vessels in harbour, on the north beach, and even on the esplanade at Glateny, to witness this "tub" affair. At about half-past five, Mr. NELSON left the north beach in a boat, with his new-fashioned ship and quacking propellers, accompanied by upwards of forty other boats, filled with men and women, and started off to the South buoy, a distance of about eight hundred yards from the pier. After some little delay, our aquatic navigator got fairly into his "tub," which was drawn by eight ducks, - himself assisting their gigantic endeavours, by moving the wheels of his vehicle; but the boats so completely crowded round him, that comparatively few persons could obtain a distinct view of this novel – and, we may add, nonsensical – concern. Shortly after six o'clock, the "tub" navigator succeeded in reaching the harbour's mouth, which put an end to his marine excursion. The weather was quite calm; had it been otherwise, it is more than probable that the "ducks", the "tub", and its tenant, would have cut but a very sorry figure on the surface of the water.

We thought on the old adage, that "one fool makes many fools" –or, perhaps, more appropriately, that a few ducks made very many a goose on the occasion. It was Mr. NELSON's benefit night, and doubtless this novel scheme was resorted to for the purpose of "raising the wind".

The Comet, Vol XVI No 58, October 5 1843

Note: 'Arthur Nelson, clown, originally with Parrish's theatrical booth, in May 1845 he was with Cooke's Circus at Yarmouth, where, in imitation of the famous clown Dicky Usher, he apparently drove four geese, pulling him in a bathtub, down the River Bure. It was a hoax but, in the crush, a suspension bridge collapsed and almost a hundred people died.' *The Victorian Clown* by Jacky Bratton & Ann Featherstone, Cambridge University Press, 2006

Imperial Eagles in Guernsey!

On Tuesday week two large birds alighted near the mill pond at Petit Bo, St Martin's. The unusual sight attracted the attention of the neighbours, who hastened to the spot, armed with stones. One of the birds flew away at the approach of their assailants; the other took to the water, where, by some mishap, it got entangled among the marshes, and, in consequence, was compelled to surrender to the two most courageous – the sons of the late Mr. PETER HEAUME, of the Falaize, in that parish, and is now to be seen at the house of its captors!

The Comet, Vol XVIII No 74, November 27 1845

Threatening Catastrophe!

In the course of last week, the steeple and great bell of St. Martin's church fell upon us; but, the bulk being more threatening than the weight, we sustained no material injury, inasmuch as that has already been repaired by the substitution of more respectable and more durable materials.

The Comet, Vol XIX No 3, March 23 1846

A BULL IN A CHINA SHOP is a subject not to be despised by the local journalist in the actual dearth of more important topics; and, though we have not to record such an event, it was almost literally fulfilled on Friday last. During the landing of cattle from a vessel in the harbour in the afternoon of that day, an ox, doubtless attracted by the splendour of the weather and the novelty of the scenery, resolved on a rural walk – or rather run – and proceeded at a rapid pace through the upper part of the town, taking Mount Durand in his route. Having indulged his perambulatory desires, Monsieur le Bœuf returned to town, when, terrified by the shouts of children great and small, he increased his pace, overturning everything and anything that impeded his progress. A few persons, we believe, were knocked down, or rather fell under the weight of the animal – without, we are happy to say, sustaining any injuries. The beast was ultimately secured, but on the following morning again played his pranks and was near placing a butcher upon the horns of a dilemma.

The Comet, Vol XX No 57, September 27 1847

Tightrope Walking

The good folks of this town and neighbourhood were put on the qui vive on Monday last, by the announcement, made in posting-bills, that CLEMENT IRVINE would, at half-past 7 o'clock in the evening of that day, perform an extraordinary feat – that of walking on a rope stretched across the harbour of St. Peter-Port, at high-water. Just previous to the appointed hour, the rain descended copiously; but, as soon as the weather cleared up, hundreds of persons collected on both piers and quays, in anticipation of witnessing the promised performance. Owing to some mismanagement, however, the hawser could not be got in proper order for the exploit. The expectant throng were, consequently, greatly disappointed; but, to counteract the disappointment, the performer promised to fulfil his engagement on the following day, at noon. The multitude, by this time, began to think they had been completely hoaxed; and very many unpleasant things were said, to the disparagement of CLEMENT IRVINE. Nevertheless, the people, ever eager after the marvellous, would not suffer themselves to be disheartened by the first check to their hopes. Hence, at the appointed hour on Tuesday, they again repaired, by thousands, to the spot already indicated. In consequence of want of proper arrangement, some further delay again occurred. Shortly before two o'clock, however, everything having been adjusted, CLEMENT IRVINE, with the assistance of his balancing-pole, ascended the rope from the deck of a foreign vessel at the north pier-head. Every eye was instantly fixed upon the performer, with alternations of hope and fear, as he moved gracefully along till he reached the shears which supported the rope on the west quay of the harbour, opposite the stores, when the beholders set up tremendous shoutings for his successful exploit. After resting a few minutes, to recruit his strength, IRVINE prepared himself to return; when again all eyes were intensely fixed upon him as he gracefully walked along till he reached the place from which he started at the first. Again his achievements were applauded, with deafening shouts from every quarter. On his return, he stood for a little while on one foot only, with as much composure as though he had been on terra firma. It is necessary to observe, that the space over which IRVINE walked was about 300 feet; and that the rope was raised from 30 to 40 feet from the bed of the harbour, which was dry at the time of this hazardous, but extraordinary feat. IRVINE was dressed in white, with a kind of red petticoat-trowsers thrown over his loins; and, that he might clearly see his way, he laid aside his hat, and appeared bareheaded, although the wind was very high at the time.

The Comet, Vol XIX No 30, June 25 1846

Plate 25: Saints Bay, Guernsey

On Thursday last, some fishermen belonging to St. Sampson, in drawing up their trawl, found a blue shark entangled therein. By dint of labour, they contrived to bring the monster into shallow water; but as they could not secure it without taking away its life, a fowling-piece was procured, and the fish shot dead in the harbour, and afterwards drawn to shore. It has since been sold to Mr. Sharshaw, druggist, who has had it skinned with the view to stuffing it, and intends presenting it to the Mechanic and Literary Society in this town. The shark measured seven feet seven inches and half from the nose to the tip of the tail. It has two formidable rows of teeth. We consider it to be a fortunate circumstance that this voracious inhabiter of the deep has been caught; otherwise, it might have proved a formidable enemy to our bathers, at this season of the year. And as some persons still continue that healthful recreation, it is right they should know that dangerous visitors of other climes sometimes find their way on our shores in search of prey, so that they may be on their guard whenever they indulge in their ablutions.

The Comet, Vol XX No 63, October 18 1847

Nocturnal Freak

During the night of Thursday last, a ladder, 38 feet in length, which had been raised at the back of Mr. Colling's house, in Bordage-street, was carried away, and thrown over the South-pier wall, where it was discovered on Friday morning. Such a ladder ordinarily requires five men to take it down; but how many were engaged in this daring nocturnal feat, we know not. We are equally ignorant of the motive that could have led the parties to play such a prank, and can attribute it to sheer wickedness.

The Comet, Vol XXI No 71, November 13 1848

"When we reflect on the various changes that fleeting time has made in the affairs of life, and are desirous of bringing to remembrance the causes that produced them, we often wonder that we have forgotten many events which may even have passed before our eyes, but which, from not having been marked by very prominent features, have glided from our memory as a tale that is told. It surely then becomes a duty to transmit to posterity occurrences which, however apparently insignificant, may yet prove important, as forming links in the chain of history. The advantage of doing so is not confined to the present age, but will certainly add to the general stock of intelligence, and form authentic materials for future history."

Annals of some of the British Norman Isles constituting the Bailiwick of Guernsey, 1831, John Jacob, Esq

INDEX *of* NAMES

Susan Ilie

Susan was born in Guernsey and works as an independent family history researcher.

Susan launched Guernsey Ancestry early in 2009 after spending several years researching her own family tree and those of friends and acquaintances. She deals with enquiries from around the world and has successfully introduced many people to their Guernsey ancestors.

During her research, Susan uncovers many long forgotten news items and stories. This book fulfils her desire to share these incredible echoes of Guernsey's past.

www.guernseyancestry.com